ISCHIA TRAVEL GUIDE

"The complete insider guide to exploring Ischia holidays, adventure, culture and festival, top tourist attraction and hidden gems."

RICHARD SMITH

TABLE OF CONTENTS

Introduction

Ischia, often called the "Emerald Isle" or the "Enchanted Isle," is a captivating gem nestled in the azure waters of the Tyrrhenian Sea, just off the picturesque Amalfi Coast of Italy. This charming island, the largest in the Gulf of Naples, is where legends come to life, where the gentle embrace of the Mediterranean sun dances with the lullaby of the sea, and where time seems to pause to savor the beauty of its landscapes.

As you step onto the shores of Ischia, you'll find yourself transported to a world where history, culture, and nature seamlessly intertwine. This verdant paradise is rich in its scenic wonders and deep, centuries-old traditions. From the moment you set foot on the island, you'll be captivated by the intoxicating aroma of lemon groves, the vibrant hues of bougainvillea, and the melodious notes of local musicians playing the accordion, serenading the setting sun.

Ischia is not just a destination; it's an experience. The island's unique blend of natural thermal springs, lush gardens, charming villages, and pristine beaches creates a tapestry of delights that beckons travelers from across the globe. Here, you can immerse yourself in rejuvenating spa therapies, savor mouthwatering Italian cuisine, and explore ancient ruins that whisper tales of a bygone era.

But Ischia is more than just a vacation spot; it's a destination for the soul. It's a place to discover the magic of hidden coves, lose yourself in meandering, cobblestone streets, and forge connections with locals proud to share their island's treasures with you. It's a place where each corner you turn reveals a new wonder, whether it's the pastel-hued facades of buildings in Forio, the breathtaking views from Mount Epomeo, or the lively atmosphere of Ischia Porto's bustling piazzas.

In this "Ischia Travel Guide," we invite you to embark on a journey to this mesmerizing island, where each moment is a postcard-worthy memory waiting to be created. Join us as we explore its history, delve into its culture, and uncover its hidden secrets. Whether you're a history enthusiast, nature lover, culinary connoisseur, or wanderer searching for life's simple pleasures, Ischia offers something that resonates with every traveler.

This enchanting island is an open invitation to embrace the dolce vita and savor the sweet life. It's a place where you can set your watch to "Ischia time" and let the waves of the Mediterranean sweep you into a world where beauty, serenity, and wonder come together. Welcome to Ischia, where the journey is as magical as the destination.

Why Visit Ischia

Ischia, the enchanting island of the Tyrrhenian Sea, holds an irresistible allure that beckons travelers worldwide. But why should you visit Ischia? What sets this island apart from the many beautiful destinations in Italy and the Mediterranean? The answer lies in a unique blend of natural wonders, cultural richness, and the ineffable charm of this Italian gem.

1. **Natural Thermal Springs:** Ischia is renowned for its natural thermal springs, bubbling up deep within the Earth for centuries. These rejuvenating waters have earned the island the nickname "L'Isola Verde" (The Green Island) due to its lush vegetation nourished by the thermal activity. Visitors can soak in thermal baths, relax in spa resorts, and experience the healing properties of Ischia's thermal waters. The island's thermal parks, like Poseidon Gardens and Negombo,

provide a surreal, tropical oasis amidst the Mediterranean.

2. Stunning Beaches: Ischia boasts an array of beautiful, diverse beaches that cater to all tastes. From the tranquil, pebbly shores of Citara to the golden sands of San Francesco Beach and the natural beauty of Maronti, there's a beach for everyone. The crystalline waters invite you to swim, snorkel, or bask in the Mediterranean sun while enjoying breathtaking coastal views.

3. Picturesque Landscapes: The island's geography is a tapestry of stunning landscapes. At its heart lies Mount Epomeo, a dormant volcano that offers panoramic views of the entire island and beyond. Verdant hills, terraced vineyards, and gardens of colorful flowers cascade down to the sea. Exploring the lush countryside, with its fragrant lemon groves and vibrant gardens, is a feast for the senses.

4. Rich History and Culture: Ischia's history can be traced back to ancient Greece, with archaeological sites like Villa Arbusto and the Castello Aragonese standing as testament to its past. The island's culture is deeply rooted in its traditions, from the centuries-old art of ceramics to the melodious sounds of the local accordion and mandolin. Visitors can immerse themselves in the daily life of Ischia's charming villages, experiencing the warmth of its people and the authenticity of its traditions.

5. Culinary Delights: Ischia's cuisine is a delectable blend of fresh seafood, local produce, and Mediterranean flavors. From traditional dishes like rabbit cacciatore and paccheri pasta to the island's renowned rabbit stew and the citrusy delight of lemon granita, Ischia offers a culinary adventure sure to tantalize your taste buds. Dining in Ischia isn't just a meal; it's an experience that connects you to the island's rich gastronomic heritage.

6. Tranquility and Relaxation: Ischia offers a respite from the hustle and bustle of daily life. Time slows down here, and the island's serene atmosphere makes it an ideal destination for relaxation and rejuvenation. Whether indulging in a spa treatment, exploring a hidden cove, or simply unwinding in a piazza with a coffee, Ischia invites you to take life more leisurely.

7. Proximity to Other Gems: Ischia's location makes it an excellent base for exploring nearby attractions such as Capri, Sorrento, the Amalfi Coast, and the archaeological wonders of Pompeii and Herculaneum. Day trips to these destinations are easily arranged from Ischia, allowing you to make the most of your time in the region.

In summary, Ischia's magnetic appeal is the product of its unique blend of nature, culture, history, and relaxation. It's a place where you can immerse yourself in the best of Italy – from its stunning landscapes to its rich heritage and sumptuous cuisine. Whether you seek adventure, relaxation, or both, Ischia offers a world of experiences waiting to be explored, making it a must-visit destination for those seeking an authentic, enchanting Italian escape.

Chapter 1: Getting to Know Ischia

Ischia, the "Emerald Isle" of Italy, is a destination that seamlessly marries the enchanting beauty of the Mediterranean with rich history, vibrant culture, and a culinary heritage that tantalizes the taste buds. Before embarking on your journey to this captivating island, it's essential to acquaint yourself with its geography and location, delve into its storied history and culture, savor the nuances of its local cuisine, and understand the language and communication that will enrich your experience.

Geography and Location:

Situated in the Tyrrhenian Sea, Ischia is the largest island in the Gulf of Naples and part of southern Italy's Campania region. Its strategic location, approximately 30 kilometers from the mainland, makes it an easily accessible paradise for travelers looking to escape the bustling cities of Naples and the Amalfi Coast.

Ischia's landscape is a testament to the geological wonders of the region. At its heart, the island is dominated by Mount Epomeo. This dormant volcano stands as the highest point on Ischia, offering spectacular vistas of the entire island and the shimmering waters surrounding it. The volcano's fertile slopes are adorned with lush vineyards, citrus groves, and picturesque villages.

The island's coastline is equally diverse, with pebbly coves, sandy beaches, and rocky cliffs awaiting exploration. Ischia's crystal-clear waters are as inviting as its lush landscapes, making it a haven for beach lovers and water enthusiasts. Thanks to its volcanic activity, the island's thermal springs provide additional allure, turning Ischia into a renowned wellness destination.

History and Culture:

Ischia's history stretches back through the annals of time. The island has seen the rise and fall of empires, and its history is an intricate tapestry woven with threads of Greek, Roman, Byzantine, and Spanish influences. You can explore this rich history in every corner of the island.

One of Ischia's most iconic historical landmarks is the Castello Aragonese. This medieval fortress rises dramatically from the sea on its islet connected to the main island by a stone bridge. The castle's storied past, from its origins as a Greek acropolis to its role as a protective fortress against marauding pirates, serves as a vivid testament to Ischia's enduring history.

While history is evident in the island's architecture and archaeological sites, Ischia's culture is a living, breathing entity that thrives daily. The local cuisine, festivals, and traditions are the pulse of the island's culture. Ischia is famous for its ceramics, a tradition passed down through generations and still a thriving art form today. These colorful, hand-painted ceramics can be found throughout the island.

The island's residents take immense pride in their musical heritage, with the accordion and mandolin being the instruments of choice. Stroll through the picturesque streets, and you might see a local musician serenading a café with melodies that have echoed through generations.

Local Cuisine:

Ischia's cuisine is a gastronomic journey through the Mediterranean, a fusion of fresh, locally sourced ingredients and traditional Italian flavors. Seafood takes center stage in Ischia's culinary scene and is expertly prepared in various regional dishes. One of the island's culinary specialties is rabbit, cooked in a rich tomato sauce, herbs, and wine to create a savory and fragrant stew.

The cuisine of Ischia also features an abundance of fresh fruits and vegetables, with a particular emphasis on sun-ripened tomatoes, aromatic basil, and luscious lemons. Pasta dishes, like the local specialty "paccheri," pair these flavors harmoniously.

Ischia's famous "Coniglio all'ischitana," or rabbit stew, is a culinary masterpiece. Slow-cooked in tomatoes, garlic, rosemary, and white wine, it's a dish that embodies the island's rich culinary tradition. The island is also renowned for its lemon-based desserts, such as the refreshing lemon granita and the decadent lemon torte. These treats are a delightful reflection of the island's abundant lemon groves.

When dining in Ischia, it's not just about the food but the entire experience. The island's charming trattorias and family-owned restaurants create an intimate atmosphere that makes every meal memorable. Dining in Ischia is about savoring each bite while enjoying the warm hospitality of the locals.

Language and Communication:

Italian is the official language of Ischia, and while many locals in the tourism industry speak some level of English, it's always appreciated when visitors attempt to communicate in Italian. Here are some basic Italian phrases that can enhance your experience on the island:

- "Ciao" – Hello
- "Grazie" – Thank you
- "Per favore" – Please
- "Buongiorno" – Good morning
- "Buonasera" – Good evening
- "Mi scusi" – Excuse me
- "Parla inglese?" – Do you speak English?
- "Sì" – Yes
- "No" – No
- "Il conto, per favore" – The bill, please

As with any travel experience, learning a few local phrases can go a long way in fostering connections with the people of Ischia and immersing yourself in the local culture.

In conclusion, Chapter 1 sets the stage for your Ischia adventure by introducing you to the island's captivating geography, deep-rooted history and culture, mouthwatering local cuisine, and the basics of language and communication. This knowledge is the foundation upon which you'll build your memorable journey through the Emerald Isle of Italy, uncovering its hidden gems and experiencing the essence of la dolce vita.

Chapter 2: Planning Your Trip

Planning your trip to Ischia is the first step in embarking on a memorable journey to this enchanting island. This chapter will guide you through the crucial aspects of preparing for your Ischia adventure. We will cover topics such as when to visit, visa and entry requirements, packing tips, and budgeting for your trip. Whether you're a seasoned traveler or your first time venturing to Italy, these insights will help ensure a smooth and enjoyable experience on the Emerald Isle.

When to Visit Ischia:

Ischia's appeal is timeless, but the best time to visit depends on your preferences and what you hope to experience on the island.

- **Spring (March to May):** Spring is a splendid time to visit Ischia. The weather is mild, and nature awakens with vibrant blossoms. This season offers a more tranquil experience, with fewer tourists and lower accommodation rates. It's an excellent time for nature enthusiasts and hikers.

- **Summer (June to August):** Summer is the peak tourist season, as travelers worldwide flock to Ischia to bask in the Mediterranean sun. The weather is warm and sunny, perfect for beachgoers. However, expect larger crowds and higher prices during this time. Booking accommodations well in advance is advisable.

- **Autumn (September to November):** Autumn is another fantastic time to visit Ischia. The weather remains pleasant, and the sea is warm for swimming. You can also enjoy the island's harvest season, savoring fresh produce and local wine. Prices start to drop, and the island becomes less crowded.

- **Winter (December to February):** Winter in Ischia is the quietest season. While it's not the best time for sunbathing, it's ideal for travelers seeking serenity, wellness, and spa experiences. You can indulge in the island's famous thermal baths and cozy up in the local trattorias.

Consider your priorities, whether they involve enjoying the buzz of summer or savoring the island's tranquility during the shoulder seasons when determining the best time to visit Ischia.

Visa and Entry Requirements:

Ischia is part of Italy and the Schengen Area, which means that the entry requirements for Ischia are the same as those for Italy. Travelers from EU countries, the United States, Canada, Australia, and many other countries are generally allowed to visit Italy for tourism purposes for up to 90 days without a visa. However, checking the latest visa and entry requirements before your trip is crucial, as regulations can change.

Ensure your passport is valid for at least six months beyond your intended departure date. Additionally, it's wise to carry a photocopy of your passport's main page and any necessary visas with you during your trip.

Packing Tips:

Packing for your trip to Ischia requires a mix of practicality and preparedness for the island's diverse activities and environments. Here are some essential packing tips to ensure you're well-prepared:

- **Clothing:** Ischia's climate calls for lightweight, breathable clothing in the summer months, including swimsuits, sun hats, and sunglasses. Remember comfortable shoes, as exploring the island often involves walking along cobblestone streets. In spring and autumn, bring layers for cooler evenings.

- **Electronics:** Electrical outlets in Italy use the European standard Type C or Type F plugs, so ensure you have the appropriate adapters for your devices. Remember your camera to capture the stunning landscapes and moments during your trip.

- **Medications and Toiletries:** If you have any essential medications, ensure you bring an adequate supply. Pharmacies are readily available on the island, but having what you need is best. Also, pack sunscreen, insect repellent, and any personal toiletries you prefer.

- **Travel Documents:** Carry printed copies of your travel itinerary, accommodation reservations, and any important contact information. Having these documents in both digital and physical forms is a good practice.

- **Reusable Water Bottle:** Staying hydrated is essential, and carrying a reusable water bottle can help minimize plastic waste and save money. Ischia's public fountains provide clean drinking water.

- **Backpack or Day Bag:** A small daypack is handy for carrying essentials when exploring the island. Having a lightweight, waterproof bag for beach days is also a good idea.

- **Language Aids:** While many Ischia locals speak some English, having a phrasebook or translation app can be handy for enhancing your interactions and experiences.

Budgeting for Your Trip:

Budgeting for your trip to Ischia can be as flexible as your travel preferences. The island offers options for various budgets, and you can tailor your experience to your financial comfort. Here are some budgeting considerations:

- **Accommodation:** Accommodation costs vary based on the type of lodging you choose, from luxury resorts to budget-friendly hostels and vacation rentals. Prices may also fluctuate seasonally, so plan accordingly.

- **Dining:** Ischia offers a range of dining options, from elegant restaurants to simple trattorias. Budget-conscious travelers can enjoy local street food and casual eateries without breaking the bank.

- **Transportation:** While Ischia's public transportation system is affordable, if you plan to explore the island extensively, consider purchasing a multi-day transport pass for convenience and savings.

- **Activities:** Ischia offers many free and low-cost activities, such as hiking, beach climbing, and exploring historic sites. Be sure to allocate some budget for entrance fees to museums, gardens, and other attractions.

- **Souvenirs:** Factor in some funds for purchasing souvenirs like ceramics, local wines, and handmade crafts to remember your Ischia adventure.

- **Extras:** Lastly, set aside a contingency fund for unexpected expenses and experiences that may arise during your trip.

In summary, Chapter 2 provides essential information for planning your trip to Ischia. By considering the best time to visit, understanding visa and entry requirements, packing strategically, and budgeting appropriately, you're well-prepared to embark on your journey to the Emerald Isle of Italy. With these details, you can focus on the exciting adventures and experiences that await on this enchanting Mediterranean island.

Chapter 3: Getting to Ischia

Getting to Ischia is integral to your journey to this captivating island. In this chapter, we will guide you through the various ways to reach Ischia, whether you're arriving by air or by sea. We'll also delve into the options for local transportation on the island and provide insights into how to get around once you've arrived. With this information at your fingertips, your arrival on the Emerald Isle of Ischia will be a seamless transition into its unique charm and allure.

Arriving by Air:

The closest major international airport to Ischia is Naples International Airport, officially known as Naples Capodichino Airport (NAP). This well-connected airport is located on the mainland, just a short distance from Naples' city center. To reach Ischia from Naples International Airport, you have several options:

1. **Ferries from Naples:** The most common way to reach Ischia from the airport is by taking a taxi or a shuttle to the nearby Naples Port, Molo Beverello, or Calata Porta di Massa. From these ports, you can catch regular ferry services to Ischia. The journey offers scenic views of the Bay of Naples. It takes approximately 45 to 90 minutes, depending on the type of ferry you choose.

2. **Hydrofoils from Naples:** Hydrofoils are a faster option for reaching Ischia from Naples. They provide a quicker journey across the bay, taking about 40 to 50 minutes. Hydrofoils are a convenient choice to reach Ischia in less time.

3. **Helicopter Transfer:** For a truly luxurious experience, you can opt for a helicopter transfer from Naples International Airport directly to Ischia. This

is the quickest way to reach the island, offering breathtaking aerial views.

Arriving by Sea:

You can arrive on Ischia by sea if you're already on the Italian mainland or exploring the Amalfi Coast. Several ports on the mainland serve as gateways to Ischia:

1. **Naples:** As mentioned earlier, Naples is the primary departure point for reaching Ischia by sea. You can catch ferries or hydrofoils from Naples' Molo Beverello or Calata Porta di Massa.

2. **Sorrento:** Sorrento, a charming town on the Amalfi Coast, offers ferry services to Ischia from the Sorrento Marina Piccola. The journey provides fantastic coastal views and takes 45 minutes to 1 hour.

3. **Amalfi and Positano:** If traveling along the Amalfi Coast, consider taking a ferry from Amalfi or Positano to Ischia. While

these routes can be a bit longer, they offer a unique way to experience the beauty of the coastline.

4. **Procida:** The neighboring island of Procida is easily accessible from Ischia. You can catch a ferry or hydrofoil from Procida to Ischia, and the short journey takes just 20 to 30 minutes.

Local Transportation:

Once you arrive in Ischia, you must navigate the island's local transportation options to explore its treasures. Here are some key methods of local transportation:

1. **Buses:** Ischia has an extensive bus network that covers the island's main destinations. The buses are a convenient way to travel between towns, beaches, and attractions. Be prepared for a leisurely journey, as the routes often meander through the picturesque landscape.

2. **Taxis:** Taxis are readily available on Ischia, and they can be an efficient way to reach your destination, especially if you're traveling in a group or with luggage. However, keep in mind that taxi fares can be relatively high on the island.

3. **Renting a Scooter or Car:** For those who want more flexibility in exploring Ischia, renting a scooter or car is an option. It's a great way to reach less accessible spots and enjoy scenic drives. Remember that parking can be a challenge in the island's busier areas.

4. **Cable Cars and Funiculars:** Ischia offers a unique mode of transportation in the form of cable cars and funiculars. For example, you can take the Funicolare di Montetiglio to ascend Mount Epomeo, rewarding you with stunning panoramic views.

Getting Around the Island:

Navigating Ischia is a delightful adventure, and the island's unique geography and diverse terrain offer various ways to explore:

1. **Walking:** Many of Ischia's towns and villages are compact and perfect for exploration on foot. Wandering through the narrow, winding streets is a charming way to soak in the local culture and atmosphere.

2. **Biking:** Cycling is a popular activity on the island, and you can rent bikes to explore at your own pace. Ischia's varied landscapes provide options for both leisurely rides and more challenging routes.

3. **Hiking:** Ischia offers fantastic hiking opportunities, with numerous trails winding through lush landscapes and leading to breathtaking viewpoints. The island's geological diversity ensures that hikers of all levels can find suitable paths.

4. **Boating:** Exploring Ischia by boat is a fantastic way to reach hidden coves, beaches, and caves. Renting a boat or joining a boat tour allows you to discover the island from a unique perspective.

In summary, Chapter 3 provides invaluable insights into getting to Ischia, whether you arrive by air or sea. It also covers local transportation options and how to navigate the island once you've landed. With this information, you'll be well-equipped to begin your Ischia adventure and make the most of your time on this captivating Mediterranean island.

Chapter 4: Where to Stay

Selecting suitable accommodation in Ischia is a crucial aspect of your journey, as it can significantly influence your overall experience on the island. In this chapter, we will explore a range of accommodation options, from luxurious resorts to cozy vacation rentals and budget-friendly alternatives. Whether you seek a tranquil escape, a romantic getaway, or a family adventure, Ischia offers diverse choices to cater to every traveler's needs.

Accommodation Options:

1. **Hotels:** Ischia boasts a wide array of hotels that cater to different tastes and budgets. From five-star luxury resorts to charming boutique hotels and family-run inns, there is a hotel for every type of traveler. Most hotels offer amenities such as pools, restaurants, and spa facilities.

2. **Resorts:** The island is renowned for its luxurious spa resorts, which often feature thermal baths, wellness centers, and stunning sea views. These resorts provide a perfect retreat for relaxation and rejuvenation.

3. **Vacation Rentals:** Vacation rentals are a popular option for those seeking a home away from home. You can choose from apartments, villas, or even traditional Ischian cottages. This type of accommodation is excellent for travelers who prefer independence and the convenience of self-catering.

4. **Bed and Breakfasts (B&Bs):** B&Bs are dotted across Ischia and offer a cozy, intimate lodging experience. These smaller establishments often have delightful hosts and a warm, family-oriented atmosphere.

5. **Agriturismi:** For a truly authentic experience, consider staying in an agriturismo. These working farms offer accommodations to guests and provide a unique opportunity to immerse yourself in the island's agricultural traditions.

6. **Camping:** Ischia offers a camping option for budget-conscious travelers. While the island doesn't have traditional campgrounds, you can find areas where camping is permitted. Remember that you may need to obtain permits for camping in specific locations.

7. **Hostels:** A few are on the island, particularly in Ischia Porto and Forio. These are budget-friendly options for solo travelers, backpackers, and those who enjoy the social atmosphere of hostels.

Recommended Hotels and Resorts:

Ischia boasts a selection of renowned hotels and resorts known for their exceptional service, stunning locations, and world-class amenities. Here are a few recommended options:

1. **Mezzatorre Resort & Spa:** This elegant resort offers a unique experience with its private beach, thermal pools, and a Michelin-starred restaurant. Located on the island's north coast, it provides breathtaking views of the sea and the Castello Aragonese.

2. **L'Albergo della Regina Isabella:** Situated in Lacco Ameno, this historic hotel has hosted celebrities and royalty over the years. It features thermal pools, a private beach, and a superb spa.

3. **San Montano Resort & Spa:** Perched on a hilltop overlooking the sea, this resort offers breathtaking views and luxurious accommodations. Guests can indulge in the

thermal park, extensive gardens, and a wellness center.

4. **Hotel Punta Molino:** Located in Ischia Porto, this boutique hotel is known for its excellent service and prime seafront location. It boasts beautiful gardens, a private beach, and thermal pools.

5. **Miramare E Castello Hotel:** Nestled in the Castello Aragonese, this enchanting hotel combines history with modern luxury. It provides unrivaled views of the castle and the sparkling sea.

Vacation Rentals and Villas:

Vacation rentals in Ischia are ideal for travelers who desire more space, privacy, and kitchen convenience. You can choose from cozy apartments to spacious villas with private gardens and pools. Some popular websites for booking vacation rentals in Ischia include Airbnb, Vrbo, and HomeAway. Whether you're looking for a romantic cottage for two or a family villa with panoramic views, you'll find a diverse range of vacation rental options.

Camping and Budget Options:

Ischia isn't known for traditional campgrounds, but camping is possible in some island regions. Camping is a budget-friendly option, particularly for those who love the outdoors. Here are a few essential tips for camping in Ischia:

- Ensure you have the necessary permits for camping in specific locations.

- Practice responsible camping and follow Leave No Trace principles.

- Be prepared for basic amenities, as campgrounds on the island may offer limited facilities.

- Camping is more feasible in the less developed and less populated parts of Ischia.

Also, hostels offer affordable accommodations in Ischia Porto and Forio for budget-conscious travelers. These hostels often provide dormitory-style rooms and a friendly atmosphere for solo travelers and backpackers.

In summary, choosing suitable accommodation in Ischia is a significant part of planning your trip. The island offers diverse options, from luxurious resorts and boutique hotels to cozy vacation rentals and budget-friendly choices like camping and hostels. Your lodging choice will shape your overall experience on Ischia, allowing you to immerse yourself in the island's beauty and culture while enjoying the comfort that suits your travel style.

Chapter 5: Exploring Ischia

Exploring Ischia is a captivating adventure that leads you through a tapestry of natural beauty, cultural heritage, and wellness experiences. In this chapter, we'll delve into the must-see attractions that define the island, uncover hidden gems off the beaten path, discover the wealth of hiking and outdoor activities available, and delve into the world of wellness and spas that make Ischia a unique destination. Whether you're an adventure seeker, a history enthusiast, or simply seeking relaxation, Ischia offers many experiences to suit your preferences.

Must-See Attractions:

1. **Castello Aragonese:** Perched on a rocky islet connected to Ischia by a stone bridge, the Castello Aragonese is an iconic attraction. This medieval fortress offers a glimpse into the island's history with its

well-preserved architecture and breathtaking sea views.

2. **Gardens of La Mortella:** Created by the famous English composer William Walton and his wife Susana, the Gardens of La Mortella are a horticultural paradise. The beautifully landscaped gardens feature exotic plants, ponds, and sculptures, all set against the backdrop of a villa that was once the Waltons' home.

3. **Maronti Beach:** One of Ischia's most renowned beaches, Maronti offers golden sands, clear waters, and charming seaside restaurants. The natural hot springs along the beach are an added attraction, allowing you to dig your thermal bath in the sand.

4. **Mount Epomeo:** The highest point on Ischia, Mount Epomeo, invites hikers to conquer its summit. The panoramic views from the top are nothing short of

spectacular, and the ascent offers opportunities to explore the island's diverse landscapes.

5. **Negombo Thermal Park:** Nestled among lush gardens, Negombo is a world-renowned thermal park with numerous pools of varying temperatures. It's a haven for relaxation and wellness, providing a rejuvenating experience.

6. **Sant'Angelo:** This picturesque fishing village on the southern coast of Ischia is a must-visit for its charming streets, colorful houses, and vibrant atmosphere. Explore its quaint harbor, boutique shops, and waterfront cafes.

7. **Villa Arbusto:** This archaeological museum offers insights into Ischia's rich history. It's home to an impressive collection of ancient artifacts, including Greek and

Roman antiquities. The villa itself is a historical gem.

Hidden Gems:

1. **Ravino Gardens:** While the Gardens of La Mortella are well-known, the Ravino Gardens are a hidden gem that will enchant plant enthusiasts. This Mediterranean garden showcases a variety of succulents and cacti in a striking setting.

2. **Soccorso Church and Beach:** Tucked away in the village of Forio, the Chiesa del Soccorso is a charming church overlooking a stunning beach. The church is a picturesque spot for photos, and the beach is a hidden oasis.

3. **Lacco Ameno's Fungo:** Lacco Ameno is known for its unique mushroom-shaped rock formation called Il Fungo. It's a fascinating natural wonder, and the nearby beach offers a tranquil escape.

4. **Sentiero Baia di Sorgeto:** Sorgeto Bay's natural hot springs are well-loved, but the Sentiero Baia di Sorgeto is a hidden gem for hikers. This coastal path offers breathtaking views and secluded spots for relaxation.

5. **Ischia Ponte:** While the Castello Aragonese draws visitors, the village of Ischia Ponte itself is a hidden treasure. Stroll through its charming streets, visit local shops, and savor delicious seafood dishes.

6. **Villa La Colombaia:** This historic villa in Forio showcases a collection of artifacts and art once owned by Luchino Visconti, the famous Italian film director. It's a unique glimpse into the world of cinema and art on the island.

Hiking and Outdoor Activities:

Ischia's diverse landscape makes it a paradise for outdoor enthusiasts. Whether you're an experienced hiker or a casual walker, there are plenty of trails and activities to explore:

1. **Hiking Trails:** Ischia offers numerous hiking trails that lead to panoramic viewpoints, hidden coves, and lush valleys. Some popular hikes include the Monte Epomeo hike, the Cava dell'Isola loop, and the Punta Imperatore trail.

2. **Water Sports:** The island's clear waters invite you to partake in various water activities, including snorkeling, scuba diving, and kayaking. The underwater world of Ischia offers colorful marine life and underwater caves to explore.

3. **Biking:** Cycling is a fantastic way to discover Ischia. You can rent bikes and explore the island's charming villages, picturesque coastlines, and scenic routes that offer magnificent sea views.

4. **Boat Tours:** Boat tours and excursions around Ischia and neighboring islands like Procida and Capri provide a unique perspective of the region's beauty. You can choose from private boat charters, group tours, and fishing excursions.

5. **Bird Watching:** Ischia's diverse landscape and protected areas offer great bird-watching opportunities. Bird enthusiasts can spot various species in the island's natural habitats.

6. **Rock Climbing:** Ischia's volcanic terrain provides an excellent environment for rock climbing. It's a fantastic option for adventure seekers with various routes catering to different experience levels.

Wellness and Spas:

Ischia's natural thermal springs have been revered for their healing properties for centuries. The island is a haven for wellness and spa experiences:

1. **Thermal Baths:** The island offers many thermal parks and baths to soak in the therapeutic waters. Venues like Poseidon Gardens and Negombo offer a variety of pools, saunas, and wellness treatments.

2. **Spa Resorts:** Many of Ischia's luxury resorts have wellness centers and spas. You can indulge in massages, facials, and other treatments on a serene seafront.

3. **Yoga and Meditation Retreats:** Ischia's serene atmosphere makes it an ideal location for yoga and meditation retreats. These retreats often occur in scenic settings, such as tranquil gardens or by the sea.

4. **Wellness Hotels:** Wellness hotels on the island offer packages that focus on relaxation, rejuvenation, and holistic well-being. These packages often include thermal baths, spa treatments, and yoga sessions.

5. **Ayurveda Centers:** Some wellness centers specialize in Ayurveda, offering ancient Indian treatments to balance the body, mind, and soul.

In conclusion, Chapter 5 takes you on a journey to explore the essence of Ischia. From must-see attractions to hidden gems, from hiking and outdoor activities to wellness and spas, the island offers an array of experiences that cater to all travelers. Embrace the beauty, culture, and wellness of Ischia as you uncover the unique charm of this Mediterranean paradise.

Chapter 6: Dining and Cuisine

Ischia's culinary scene is a delightful blend of Mediterranean flavors, traditional Italian cuisine, and unique local dishes. In this chapter, we will take you on a culinary journey to explore the island's local dishes and delicacies, introduce you to popular restaurants and eateries, delve into dining etiquette in Ischia, and reveal the joyous world of food festivals that celebrate the island's gastronomic treasures.

Local Dishes and Delicacies:

1. **Coniglio all'Ischitana:** Ischia's most famous dish is Coniglio all'Ischitana, a rabbit stew cooked in tomatoes, garlic, rosemary, and white wine. This savory and aromatic dish is a culinary masterpiece that embodies the island's rich food tradition.

2. **Risotto all'Ischitana:** This delightful risotto is made with locally caught seafood,

typically a combination of shrimp, mussels, and clams, along with a fragrant blend of tomatoes, garlic, and parsley.

3. **Paccheri:** Paccheri is a type of pasta that's popular in Ischia. These large, tube-like pasta shapes are often served with fresh seafood, tomatoes, and basil, creating a flavorful and satisfying dish.

4. **Sarde a Beccafico:** This traditional dish features sardines stuffed with breadcrumbs, pine nuts, and raisins, then rolled and baked. The sweet and savory combination is a true Ischian delicacy.

5. **Limoncello:** Ischia's abundant lemon groves provide Limoncello's key ingredient: a sweet and tangy lemon liqueur. Enjoy a glass of Limoncello as a refreshing digestif after your meal.

6. **Capperi di Pantelleria:** Ischia is known for its exceptional capers. It is often found in

local dishes as a flavorful and slightly pungent garnish.

Popular Restaurants:

1. **Ristorante Da Ciccio:** Located in Forio, this family-run restaurant is renowned for its seafood dishes, including the delicious Risotto all'Ischitana. The warm hospitality and waterfront location make it a favorite among locals and tourists.

2. **Il Mosaico:** Situated within the L'Albergo della Regina Isabella, Il Mosaico is a Michelin-starred restaurant that offers a gastronomic journey of Italian and Mediterranean cuisine. The exceptional seafood and wines make it an unforgettable dining experience.

3. **Il Ghiottone:** This charming restaurant in Ischia Porto is famous for its Coniglio all'Ischitana and other traditional Ischian

dishes. The warm and welcoming ambiance is enhanced by live accordion music.

4. **Lo Scoglio:** Found in the fishing village of Sant'Angelo, Lo Scoglio is renowned for its fresh seafood. Dine on the terrace overlooking the bay and savor dishes like spaghetti with sea urchins and grilled fish.

5. **Ristorante Pietratorcia:** In the heart of Forio, Ristorante Pietratorcia is celebrated for its flavorful paccheri dishes and locally sourced ingredients. The restaurant's warm atmosphere and extensive wine list complement the delicious cuisine.

Dining Etiquette:

Dining in Ischia is an experience that combines delicious food with Italian hospitality. Here are some tips to enhance your dining experience and show respect for local customs:

1. **Reservations:** It's a good practice to make reservations, especially at popular

restaurants, as they can get busy, especially during the tourist season.

2. **Dress Code:** While Ischia is a relaxed destination, it's courteous to dress neatly when dining in nicer restaurants. Casual attire is generally acceptable but avoid beachwear.

3. **Tipping:** Tipping is appreciated but not obligatory. A service charge is sometimes included in the bill, but it's common to leave small change or round up the total.

4. **Pace of Dining:** Italian meals are meant to be savored, so don't rush through your food. Enjoy the conversation and the flavors of your dishes.

5. **Local Wine:** Ischia produces excellent wines. Ask your server for recommendations on pairing the right local wine with your meal.

6. **Fruit After the Meal:** It's customary in Italy to enjoy fruit as a dessert after a meal. Consider trying some of the island's delightful fresh fruits.

Food Festivals:

Ischia hosts various food festivals that showcase the island's culinary heritage and celebrate its unique dishes. Here are a few notable ones:

1. **Sagra del Coniglio all'Ischitana:** This festival, dedicated to the island's famous rabbit dish, is held in Ischia Porto. It's an opportunity to savor the finest Coniglio all'Ischitana and other local dishes.

2. **Festival of Sant'Anna:** In Forio, the Festival of Sant'Anna combines religious and culinary celebrations. Local food vendors set up stalls in the streets, offering a taste of traditional Ischian dishes.

3. **Festa del Mare:** Celebrated in Sant'Angelo, the Festa del Mare is a

delightful seafood festival. You can sample various fresh seafood dishes while enjoying live music and dancing.

4. **L'IschiaGusto:** This annual food festival in Ischia Porto features a market of local and regional products, allowing you to savor and purchase the island's finest food and wine.

5. **Chestnut Festival:** Held in Fontana, this autumn festival celebrates the harvest of chestnuts with traditional music, dances, and an abundance of chestnut-based treats.

In summary, Chapter 6 immerses you in the culinary delights of Ischia. From the island's local dishes and delicacies to popular restaurants that serve them, dining etiquette, and the joyous food festivals that celebrate Ischia's gastronomic treasures, your taste buds will be on a delightful journey throughout your stay. Savor the Mediterranean flavors and experience Ischian cuisine's heart and soul.

Chapter 7: Shopping and Souvenirs

Ischia offers a delightful shopping experience with many unique and locally crafted products. In this chapter, we will explore what to buy in Ischia, the best shopping areas to find these treasures, the charm of local markets, and provide you with some bargaining tips to make the most of your shopping adventures on the island.

What to Buy in Ischia:

1. **Ceramics:** Ischia is renowned for its exquisite ceramic creations. You can find colorful tiles, pottery, and various shapes and sizes of decorative items. These handcrafted ceramics often feature traditional motifs, such as lemons, flowers, and marine themes.

2. **Limoncello:** Ischia's bountiful lemon groves yield some of the best lemons in Italy, making Limoncello a sought-after souvenir.

This lemon liqueur is a delightful, sweet-and-tangy spirit that encapsulates the essence of the island.

3. **Local Wines:** Ischia boasts several wineries that produce unique and high-quality wines. Aglianico, Forastera, and Biancolella are some of the varietals you can explore. Consider purchasing a few bottles to take home and savor.

4. **Capri Pants:** The elegant and timeless Capri pants, known as "Capri pants," are popular in Ischia. These comfortable, stylish trousers are perfect for the Mediterranean climate.

5. **Coral Jewelry:** The waters surrounding Ischia are teeming with coral, and the island is known for its exquisite coral jewelry. Look for intricate pieces like necklaces, earrings, and bracelets.

6. **Herbs and Spices:** Ischia's lush landscape yields a variety of herbs and spices. Consider buying locally produced herbs like rosemary, oregano, and bay leaves to enhance your culinary creations.

Best Shopping Areas:

1. **Ischia Porto:** The main town of Ischia Porto offers numerous shops, boutiques, and local artisans. The Corso Vittoria Colonna is a bustling street with various stores, and the pedestrian area along the marina is a pleasant place for leisurely shopping.

2. **Forio:** Forio, the second-largest town on the island, is known for its charming streets lined with shops selling everything from ceramics to fashion. The Corso Matteo Verde is a famous shopping street.

3. **Sant'Angelo:** This picturesque village on the southern coast of Ischia offers unique

boutiques and shops selling local crafts, fashion, and souvenirs. The winding streets and boutique stores make shopping in Sant'Angelo a charming experience.

4. **Lacco Ameno:** Lacco Ameno is a favorite spot for high-end shopping. The town boasts designer boutiques and jewelry shops along its elegant streets.

5. **Casamicciola:** This town is known for its thermal waters and artisanal shops. Stroll along its streets to discover local products and unique souvenirs.

Local Markets:

1. **Mercato Ittico (Fish Market):** In Ischia Porto, the Mercato Ittico is a vibrant fish market where you can observe the day's local catch. It's an ideal place to buy fresh seafood or enjoy the lively atmosphere.

2. **Mercato Comunale (Municipal Market):** Located in Ischia Porto, this

market is a treasure trove of local produce, including fruits, vegetables, cheeses, and herbs. It's a great spot to immerse yourself in the island's culinary traditions.

3. **Mercato di Forio:** In Forio, this market offers an array of goods, from fresh food to clothing and accessories. It's a bustling market where you can find various local products.

Bargaining Tips:

Bargaining is rare in most Ischian shops, especially in established stores and boutiques. However, there are some tips to keep in mind when shopping on the island:

1. **Markets and Street Vendors:** Bargaining is more acceptable in local markets and with street vendors. In such cases, you can politely ask for a lower price or inquire if they can offer any

discounts, especially when purchasing multiple items.

2. **Politeness and Respect:** Approach bargaining with politeness and respect. The aim is to find a mutually agreeable price, not to haggle aggressively.

3. **Cash Payments:** Many small shops and street vendors may prefer cash payments. Having cash on hand can sometimes lead to more flexible negotiations.

4. **Purchases in Bulk:** If you plan to buy multiple items from the same vendor, inquire if they can offer a package deal or a discount for a bulk purchase.

5. **Compare Prices:** Before bargaining, explore a few different shops or stalls to understand the general price range for the items you want to buy. This will give you a better sense of what's a fair price.

6. **Be Willing to Walk Away:** If you're unsatisfied with the price, be prepared to walk away. Sometimes, vendors may be more willing to negotiate when they see potential customers leaving.

7. **Enjoy the Experience:** Bargaining in local markets can be a fun and engaging part of your shopping experience. Embrace it as an opportunity to interact with locals and learn about their culture.

In conclusion, shopping in Ischia offers a delightful exploration of the island's unique products and crafts. From ceramics and Limoncello to coral jewelry and herbs, there are plenty of treasures to discover. Explore the charming shopping areas and local markets, and remember that while bargaining may not be common in all settings, it can be a part of your shopping experience in specific situations.

Chapter 8: Nightlife and Entertainment

Ischia, renowned for its natural beauty and relaxation, also offers vibrant nightlife and entertainment options that cater to various tastes. In this chapter, we will delve into the island's nightlife scene, including bars and nightclubs, the excitement of live music and shows, the rich cultural events that add depth to Ischia's offerings, and the colorful festivals and celebrations that light up the nights.

Bars and Nightclubs:

1. **Piazza degli Eroi (Heroes' Square):** This lively square in Ischia Porto is a popular gathering place for locals and visitors. You'll find a mix of bars and cafes, perfect for sipping cocktails or enjoying a nightcap. The atmosphere is festive, especially during the summer months.

2. **Bar dell'Arte:** Situated in the heart of Forio, Bar dell'Arte is a fashionable lounge bar known for its creative cocktails, live music, and art exhibitions. It's an ideal place to unwind and mingle with a chic crowd.

3. **Blubar:** Found in Lacco Ameno, Blubar offers a stylish setting to enjoy cocktails and music. The bar often hosts DJ nights and dance parties that continue late into the night.

4. **Florio's Wine Bar:** If you appreciate a fine wine selection, Florio's Wine Bar in Forio is the place to be. It offers an extensive list of wines, both local and international, along with a cozy atmosphere.

5. **Café del Mar:** Located on the waterfront in Ischia Porto, Café del Mar is a laid-back beachfront bar with a relaxed vibe. It's the perfect spot to sip aperitifs and enjoy sunset views.

6. **Cava dell'Isola:** This iconic nightclub in Ischia Porto is known for its vibrant nightlife. Cava dell'Isola offers an unforgettable party experience with various dance floors and music styles.

Live Music and Shows:

1. **Teatro di Ischia:** The island's main theater, Teatro di Ischia, hosts various cultural events, including classical concerts, theater performances, and ballet shows. It's a beautiful venue for experiencing high-quality artistic presentations.

2. **Café Teatro**: Found in the charming village of Sant'Angelo, Café Teatro offers a combination of live music, comedy, and artistic performances. Enjoy a dinner show or savor a cocktail while watching a live act.

3. **Local Music in Bars:** Many bars in Ischia feature live music, particularly during the summer season. It's common to find local

bands or musicians playing traditional and contemporary tunes.

4. **Open-air concerts:** During the summer, open-air concerts are frequently held in various towns on the island. These events offer an opportunity to enjoy music in scenic settings, from piazzas to seaside locations.

Cultural Events:

1. **Ischia Global Film & Music Festival:** This annual event celebrates cinema and music. It features film screenings, musical performances, and the opportunity to interact with industry professionals.

2. **Summer Arts Festival:** Ischia's Summer Arts Festival offers diverse cultural events, from art exhibitions to poetry readings and performances. It takes place in various locations on the island.

3. **Ischia Invita:** A literary festival that brings writers, poets, and intellectuals together to discuss literature and culture. It's a fascinating event for book enthusiasts and intellectual discourse enthusiasts.

4. **Exhibitions and Art Galleries:** Ischia has a growing art scene, with several art galleries hosting shows and cultural events throughout the year. These galleries often showcase the works of both local and international artists.

Festivals and Celebrations:

1. **Festa di Sant'Anna:** Celebrated in late July, the Festa di Sant'Anna is a significant religious and cultural event in Ischia. It includes processions, fireworks, and various festivities throughout the island.

2. **Sant'Angelo's Feast:** In August, Sant'Angelo holds its annual feast, featuring a procession with a statue of the village's

patron saint. The streets are adorned with lights, and the celebration culminates with a spectacular fireworks display over the sea.

3. **Easter Celebrations:** Ischia's Easter celebrations are deeply rooted in local tradition. The island's towns come alive with processions, musical performances, and religious events during Holy Week.

4. **Ferragosto:** On August 15th, Italians celebrate Ferragosto, a holiday that marks the peak of summer. Ischia hosts various events, including fireworks displays, concerts, and beach parties.

5. **New Year's Eve:** Ischia welcomes the new year enthusiastically and celebrates. The island's towns light up with fireworks, parties, and live music. It's a fantastic way to start the year with joy and festivity.

In summary, Chapter 8 introduces you to Ischia's vibrant nightlife and entertainment offerings.

From bars and nightclubs to live music and shows, cultural events, and the island's colorful festivals and celebrations, there's no shortage of entertainment options to suit your preferences. Whether you're seeking a night of dancing, cultural enrichment, or simply enjoying the local festivities, Ischia has something for everyone to enjoy after the sun sets.

Chapter 9: Practical Information

While Ischia is a paradise for travelers, it's essential to be well-prepared and informed about practical matters to ensure a safe and enjoyable stay. In this chapter, we'll provide you with valuable practical information, including safety tips, health and medical services, money and currency exchange, and internet and communication, to help you confidently navigate the island.

Safety Tips:

1. **Swimming and Water Safety:** While Ischia offers beautiful beaches and clear waters, it's essential to exercise caution when swimming. Pay attention to the currents and follow any safety flags or signs. Consider wearing a life jacket if you need to be a stronger swimmer.

2. **Sun Protection:** The Mediterranean sun can be intense, so always use sunscreen with a high SPF, wear a wide-brimmed hat, and protect your eyes with sunglasses. Stay hydrated and seek shade during the hottest part of the day.

3. **Road Safety:** If you plan to rent a scooter or drive on the island, be aware that Ischia's roads can be narrow and winding. Drive cautiously, wear helmets on a scooter, and follow local traffic rules.

4. **Watch Your Belongings:** While Ischia is generally a safe destination, keeping an eye on your belongings is a good practice, especially in crowded places like markets and public transport.

5. **Emergency Numbers:** In case of an emergency, dial 112 for general emergencies, 113 for the police, and 115 for the fire department.

6. **Local Customs and Etiquette:** Familiarize yourself with local customs and etiquette. In churches, for example, modest dress is expected. It's also polite to greet locals with a friendly "Buongiorno" or "Buonasera."

Health and Medical Services:

1. **Pharmacies:** Ischia has numerous pharmacies (farmacie) that offer a wide range of over-the-counter medications and health products. Most pharmacies post a list of after-hours pharmacies for emergencies.

2. **Hospitals and Medical Centers:** Ischia has several medical facilities and hospitals. The main hospital, Rizzoli Hospital, is in Lacco Ameno, but there are smaller medical centers across the island. The European Health Insurance Card (EHIC) is generally accepted.

3. **Travel Insurance:** It's advisable to have comprehensive travel insurance that covers medical emergencies, trip cancellations, lost luggage, and other unforeseen situations.

4. **Pharmacies on Duty:** Pharmacies in Italy follow a rotating schedule for after-hours service. You can find a list of pharmacies on duty in your area posted on the door of the nearest pharmacy.

5. **Water and Food Safety:** Tap water in Ischia is generally safe. However, bottled water is widely available if you prefer. Enjoy the local cuisine confidently, as restaurants adhere to strict food safety standards.

Money and Currency Exchange:

1. **Currency:** The currency in Italy is the Euro (€). You can withdraw cash from ATMs throughout the island, and credit cards are widely accepted in hotels, restaurants, and shops.

2. **Currency Exchange:** While there are currency exchange offices in Ischia, it's often more convenient to withdraw Euros from ATMs, which typically offer competitive exchange rates.

3. **Banks:** Banks on the island are generally open from Monday to Friday, with a break during the middle of the day. ATMs are available outside of bank hours.

4. **Tipping:** Tipping is appreciated but not obligatory. It's customary to leave small change or round up the bill in restaurants and cafes. For exceptional service, you can leave a tip of about 10%.

5. **Currency Converter Apps:** Consider using currency converter apps on your smartphone to check exchange rates and calculate prices in your preferred currency.

Internet and Communication:

1. **Internet Access:** Most hotels, restaurants, and cafes in Ischia offer free Wi-Fi to their customers. You can also find internet points and internet cafes for a fee.

2. **Mobile Coverage:** Ischia has good mobile phone coverage, and you can easily purchase a local SIM card for your unlocked phone if you wish to have a local number for calls and data.

3. **Emergency Numbers:** In case of a medical emergency or if you need police or fire department assistance, dial the appropriate emergency number: 112 for general emergencies, 113 for the police, and 115 for the fire department.

4. **Postal Services:** You can send postcards and letters from Ischia's post offices (Ufficio Postale). Postal services are generally

available on weekdays, and you can purchase stamps and mail your items there.

5. **Language:** While Italian is the official language, many locals in Ischia's tourist areas understand and speak English, especially in hotels, restaurants, and shops. Learning a few basic Italian phrases can be helpful and appreciated.

6. **Time Zone:** Ischia follows Central European Time (CET) during standard time and Central European Summer Time (CEST) during daylight saving time. Be sure to check the local time when planning your activities.

7. **Electricity:** Ischia uses the Europlug Type C and Type F sockets. You may need a plug adapter if your devices have a different plug type.

In conclusion, practical information is crucial to ensure a smooth and enjoyable visit to Ischia.

Adhering to safety tips, being aware of health and medical services, understanding money and currency exchange, and staying connected with the internet and communication are vital aspects of your travel preparations. With the proper knowledge and practice, you can make the most of your journey to this stunning Mediterranean destination.

Chapter 10: Travel Tips and Resources

As you prepare for your Ischia adventure, equipping yourself with essential travel tips and resources will enhance your journey. In this chapter, we'll cover crucial aspects of travel, including the importance of travel insurance, the value of language and communication apps, tips for planning your itinerary, and sustainable travel practices to respect the environment and culture of this beautiful island.

Travel Insurance:

1. **Why You Need Travel Insurance:** Travel insurance is a vital safety net that provides financial protection against unexpected events. It can cover medical emergencies, trip cancellations, lost luggage, and other unforeseen situations that may disrupt your plans.

2. **Medical Coverage:** Ensure your travel insurance includes comprehensive medical coverage, covering doctor visits, hospitalization, and emergency medical evacuations. Verify if your policy covers pre-existing conditions.

3. **Trip Cancellation and Interruption:** Look for a policy that provides coverage in case you need to cancel or interrupt your trip due to unforeseen circumstances such as illness, natural disasters, or other emergencies.

4. **Lost or Delayed Luggage:** Opt for coverage compensating you for lost or delayed luggage. This can be essential, especially when traveling with valuable items.

5. **Adventurous Activities:** If you plan on partaking in adventurous activities such as

hiking, water sports, or rock climbing, make sure your insurance covers these activities.

6. **Compare Policies:** Shop around and compare travel insurance policies to find the one that best suits your needs and budget.

Language and Communication Apps:

1. **Language Learning Apps:** Learning basic Italian phrases can greatly enhance the travel experience. Apps like Duolingo, Babbel, or Rosetta Stone can help you acquire language skills before your trip.

2. **Translation Apps:** Translation apps like Google Translate can be invaluable for quick translations and communication. You can even use your phone's camera to translate text in real-time.

3. **Navigation Apps:** Download navigation apps like Google Maps or Maps. me to help you navigate Ischia and its winding streets.

These apps often work offline, which can be helpful with limited connectivity.

4. **Messaging Apps:** WhatsApp is widely used in Italy for communication. It's an excellent way to stay in touch with friends and family back home and communicate with locals if necessary.

5. **Local SIM Cards:** If you want a local number for calls and data, consider purchasing a local SIM card when you arrive in Ischia. This can be convenient for staying connected during your stay.

Itinerary Planning:

1. **Ischia's Main Attractions:** Identify the main attractions you want to visit, such as Castello Aragonese, Maronti Beach, and Mount Epomeo. Research their opening hours and any admission fees.

2. **Exploring Off the Beaten Path:** While the popular attractions are a must-see,

consider exploring the lesser-known parts of Ischia, like hidden beaches, charming villages, and local markets.

3. **Activity and Tour Planning:** Plan specific activities and excursions, whether it's hiking, diving, or a boat tour. Consider booking tours in advance to secure your spot, especially during peak tourist seasons.

4. **Dining Reservations:** If there are particular restaurants you want to experience, make reservations in advance, especially at high-end or popular establishments.

5. **Local Events and Festivals:** Check for local events, festivals, or cultural happenings during your visit. These can provide you with unique insights into the local culture.

6. **Pack Smart:** Pack according to the season and your planned activities. Remember

essentials like sunscreen, comfortable shoes, and a reusable water bottle.

Sustainable Travel:

1. **Respect the Environment:** Ischia's natural beauty is a treasure, so be mindful of your environmental impact. Dispose of your waste responsibly, use reusable bags, and avoid single-use plastics.

2. **Support Local Economy:** Choose local businesses, restaurants, and products to support the island's economy. Buying locally-made souvenirs and dining at family-run restaurants can contribute to the community.

3. **Conserve Water and Energy:** Be conscious of water and energy usage, especially on an island with limited resources. Use water sparingly and turn off lights and air conditioning when not needed.

4. **Respect Local Culture:** Familiarize yourself with local customs and traditions, and respect residents' way of life. Dress modestly in churches and cultural sites.

5. **Leave No Trace:** Practice the Leave No Trace principles when enjoying Ischia's natural beauty. Pack out what you bring in and avoid damaging the environment.

6. **Use Public Transportation:** Ischia offers a reliable and eco-friendly public transportation system. Consider using buses, trams, and boats to explore the island, reducing your carbon footprint.

7. **Stay in Eco-Friendly Accommodations:** Look for eco-friendly hotels and accommodations prioritizing sustainability and responsible tourism practices.

In conclusion, a well-prepared traveler is likelier to have a memorable and enjoyable experience in

Ischia. Travel insurance ensures peace of mind, language and communication apps enhance your interaction ability, itinerary planning maximizes your time, and sustainable travel practices help protect the island's unique environment and culture. These resources and tips will contribute to your enjoyment of Ischia and demonstrate your commitment to responsible and respectful travel.

Chapter 11: Sample Itineraries

Creating a memorable itinerary for your visit to Ischia is a delightful task. This chapter provides sample itineraries catering to different interests and duration of stay on the island. Whether planning a weekend getaway or an extended vacation, these sample itineraries will help you make the most of your time in this Mediterranean gem.

Sample 1: A Relaxing Weekend Getaway

Day 1: Arrival and Unwinding

- Morning: Arrive at Naples International Airport (NAP) and take a hydrofoil or ferry to Ischia. Check into your chosen accommodation.

- Afternoon: Spend your first day at the beach. Maronti Beach is a serene choice. Relax under the sun, swim in the clear waters, and enjoy a beachside lunch.

- Evening: Stroll through the streets of Ischia Porto, enjoy a traditional Italian dinner at a local restaurant, and savor some limoncello.

Day 2: Exploring Ischia's Charm

- Morning: Visit the Castello Aragonese, a medieval castle perched on a rocky islet. Explore its history and take in panoramic views of the island.

- Lunch: Enjoy a seafood lunch at a seaside restaurant near the castle.

- Afternoon: Explore the charming village of Sant'Angelo. Wander its cobblestone streets and relax on its sandy beaches.

- Evening: Return to Ischia Porto for dinner. Try a local dish like Coniglio all'Ischitana.

Day 3: Nature and Departure

- Morning: Take a hike to the summit of Mount Epomeo for breathtaking views. For a more relaxed morning, consider visiting the beautiful Giardini La Mortella, a garden created by English composer William Walton.

- Lunch: Savor a Mediterranean lunch at a restaurant with a view.

- Afternoon: Spend your last moments on the island at a spa or by the beach, depending on your preferences.

- Evening: Catch a ferry back to Naples to end your weekend getaway in Ischia.

Sample 2: A Week of Cultural Exploration

Day 1: Arrival and Ischia Porto

- Morning: Arrive in Ischia and check into your hotel in Ischia Porto. Take a leisurely walk along the marina and enjoy a seaside lunch.

- Afternoon: Visit the Castello Aragonese to learn about Ischia's history and enjoy panoramic views.

- Evening: Dine at a traditional Ischian restaurant in Ischia Porto.

Day 2: Forio and La Mortella Gardens

- Morning: Explore the town of Forio, with its beautiful churches, bustling market, and charming streets.

- Lunch: Have lunch at a local trattoria in Forio.

- Afternoon: Visit the stunning Giardini La Mortella, known for its botanical beauty and musical legacy.

- Evening: Return to Ischia Porto for dinner and evening relaxation.

Day 3: Sant'Angelo and Thermal Baths

- Morning: Head to the picturesque village of Sant'Angelo, known for its charm and idyllic setting.

- Lunch: Savor fresh seafood at a seaside restaurant in Sant'Angelo.

- Afternoon: Spend the afternoon at the thermal baths or wellness center in Sant'Angelo, indulging in spa treatments.

- Evening: Enjoy a relaxed dinner at a local restaurant.

Day 4: Outdoor Adventures

- Morning: Take a guided hike to the summit of Mount Epomeo, where you'll enjoy spectacular views.

- Lunch: Relish a packed picnic lunch on the mountain or return to town for a meal.

- Afternoon: Explore the beaches and go snorkeling in the clear waters.

- Evening: Dine by the beach and unwind.

Day 5: Casamicciola and Thermal Baths

- Morning: Explore Casamicciola, known for its thermal waters and lush landscapes.

- Lunch: Have lunch at a local eatery in town.

- Afternoon: Enjoy the healing properties of Ischia's thermal baths at a nearby spa.

- Evening: Head back to Ischia Porto for dinner.

Day 6: A Day at the Beach and Shopping

- Morning: Enjoy a leisurely morning at the beach, such as Maronti Beach or Citara Beach.

- Lunch: Savor a seafood lunch at a beachside restaurant.

- Afternoon: Shop for local souvenirs, such as ceramics and Limoncello, in Ischia Porto.

- Evening: Dine at a local pizzeria and enjoy traditional Italian pizza.

Day 7: Departure and Final Relaxation

- Morning: Enjoy a spa treatment or leisurely breakfast by the sea during your last morning.

- Lunch: Have a farewell lunch at a waterfront restaurant.

- Afternoon: Relax on the beach or dip in the thermal waters.

- Evening: Depart from Ischia carrying cherished memories of your week of cultural exploration.

These sample itineraries offer a starting point for planning your Ischia adventure. Tailor them to your preferences and interests, and embrace the opportunity to immerse yourself in this beautiful Mediterranean island's rich culture, stunning landscapes, and tranquil ambiance. Whether it's a weekend getaway or an extended stay, Ischia promises a memorable and relaxing experience.

Conclusion

Your journey through the Ischia Travel Guide has taken you on a captivating voyage to a Mediterranean paradise where nature's wonders, rich history, and vibrant culture converge to create an experience unlike any other. As you reach the end of this guide, you've gained the knowledge and insights needed to embark on a remarkable adventure to Ischia. This island promises to enchant your senses and touch your soul.

With its pristine beaches, lush landscapes, and therapeutic thermal springs, Ischia offers a haven for relaxation and rejuvenation. Its picturesque villages, ancient castles, and churches invite you to explore its rich history and vibrant culture. The delightful aroma of Italian cuisine, from fresh seafood to delectable pastries, will tantalize your taste buds, ensuring that your culinary journey is as memorable as the island's stunning scenery.

While the beauty of Ischia is abundant, so are the opportunities for adventure. Whether hiking to the summit of Mount Epomeo, diving into crystal-clear waters, or taking a stroll through charming villages, you'll be immersed in the island's natural wonders. The warmth and hospitality of the Ischian people will make you feel right at home as you experience the authenticity and charm of this remarkable destination.

In your journey through the chapters of this guide, you've explored the geography, history, and culture of Ischia. You've discovered the secrets of local cuisine, learned about language and communication, and gathered practical information to enhance your stay. You've considered the importance of travel insurance, language and communication apps, itinerary planning, and sustainable travel practices as you prepare for your adventure.

Sample itineraries have offered you a taste of Ischia's diverse experiences, whether you're seeking a relaxing weekend escape or an immersive cultural exploration over a week. The itineraries provide a starting point for creating your unique adventure tailored to your interests and preferences.

As you embark on your journey to Ischia, remember the island's timeless beauty, the warmth of its people, and the serenity that awaits you. Ischia invites you to immerse yourself in its natural wonders, indulge in its culinary delights, and discover its rich history. It promises relaxation and adventure, tradition and modernity, all within the embrace of the azure Mediterranean.

Embrace the magic of Ischia, where time seems to slow down, and the essence of Italy is distilled into an island that offers equal serenity, beauty, and authenticity. Whether you're seeking a tranquil escape, a cultural exploration, or a bit of both, Ischia awaits your arrival with open arms.

As you embark on your journey, remember that Ischia is not merely a destination; it's an experience that will linger in your heart and memory long after you've left its shores. So go forth, explore, savor, and soak in the beauty of Ischia, and may your travels be filled with joy, wonder, and a profound sense of connection with this magical island.

Bon viaggio and arrivederci!

Printed in Great Britain
by Amazon

40249791R00056